Kittens

A very first picture book

Consultant: Nicola Tuxworth

LORENZ BOOKS

Let's play
tag.

You can't
catch me!

What's
this?

Got it
this time!

I can see you ...

... and I'm going
to get you! I'm
a spotted leopard
in the jungle.

Can I eat it?

We're really hungry.

Wait for
me!

There's lunch.
Let's go!

Now for a bath ...

... and a
scratch.

That
was a
nice
nap.

I'm sure
that
wasn't
there
before ...

I'd better
investigate.

I wonder
what this
is for?

Can I
climb *up*
it ...

... or *through* it?

What a busy day
we've had.

It's time
for bed.

First published in 1996 by Lorenz Books
an imprint of Anness Publishing Limited
27 West 20th Street
New York, NY 10011

Reprinted in 1997, 1998

LORENZ BOOKS are available for bulk purchase
for sales promotion and for premium use.
For details write or call the sales director,
Lorenz Books, 27 West 20th Street, New York,
NY 10011; (800) 354-9657

1SBN 1 85967 246 9

Publisher: Joanna Lorenz
Senior Children's Books Editor:
    Sue Grabham
Editor: Sophie Warne
Photography: Lucy Tizard
Design and Typesetting:
    Michael Leaman Design Partnership
Picture credits: Solitaire Photographic/Angela
    Rixon: pp. 8–9; 20–21.

The Publishers would like to thank the North
London Shelter of the Cat's Protection League
for supplying the kittens who appear in
this book.

Printed in Hong Kong/China

10 9 8 7 6 5 4 3